THE REVOLUTIONARY WAR

WAR

Why They Fought

BY KRISTIN MARCINIAK

CONTENT CONSULTANT
Robert J. Allison, PhD
Chair, History
Suffolk University

COMPASS POINT BOOKS
a capstone imprint

Compass Point Books are published by Capstone,
1710 Roe Crest Drive, North Mankato, Minnesota 56003
www.capstonepub.com

Editorial Credits
Mari Kesselring, editor; Maggie Villaume, designer; Nikki Farinella, production specialist; Catherine Neitge and Ashlee Suker, consulting editor and designer

Image Credits
Corbis: 35, Bettmann, cover, 10, Tarker, 31; Library of Congress: 20, 25, 33, 58, Charles E. Mills/Detroit Publishing Company, 40, Currier & Ives, 28, 45, 59, François Godefroy, 16, Henry Alexander Ogden, 23, Illman Brothers, 51, John Dixon, 8, Matthew Darly, 46, Pierre Gabriel Berthault, 56, P.S. Duval & Co., 27, Robert Pollard, 19, Robert Sayer and John Bennett, 13, Thomas Paine, 29; North Wind Picture Archives, 7, 11, 14, 21, 37, 39, 42, 47, 49, 53, 57; Shutterstock Images: 5, Zack Frank, 17

Library of Congress Cataloging-in-Publication Data
Marciniak, Kristin.
  The Revolutionary War : why they fought / by Kristin Marciniak.
      pages cm.—(What Were They Fighting For?)
  Includes bibliographical references and index.
  ISBN 978-0-7565-5169-8 (hardcover)
  ISBN 978-0-7565-5173-5 (paperback)
  ISBN 978-0-7565-5181-0 (ebook pdf)
  1. United States—History—Revolution, 1775–1783—Juvenile literature. 2. United States—History—Revolution, 1775–1783—Causes—Juvenile literature. 3. United States—Politics and government—To 1775—Juvenile literature. 4. Great Britain—Politics and government—1760–1789—Juvenile literature. 5. World politics—18th century. 6. Globalization—Juvenile literature. I. Title.
  E208.M339 2015
  973.3—dc23   2014047997

Printed in Canada.
032015   008825FRF15

TABLE OF CONTENTS

CHAPTER ONE
PREWAR
Politics

The American Revolutionary War began in 1775. But the seeds of rebellion were planted a decade earlier. It was 1765, two years after the French and Indian War ended. Great Britain had forced France out of North America to protect its 13 colonies. As a result of the war, American Indian tribes had been pushed westward. The eastern part of North America belonged entirely to King George III and the British crown.

It was an important victory for the British. But it was also a costly one. The French and Indian War cost nearly $13 billion in today's dollars.

The British spent a large portion of that money defending North America. King George III and his advisers thought the colonies should repay a portion of the debt. One of the easiest ways to do that was by raising taxes on purchased goods in the colonies.

Previously the colonies—Connecticut, Delaware, Georgia, Maryland, Massachusetts, New Hampshire, New Jersey, New York, North Carolina, Pennsylvania, Rhode Island, South Carolina, and Virginia—had mostly governed themselves. Even though they were part of the British Empire, individual colonies

King George III ruled the British Empire.

managed local matters on their own. Colonies took care of such things as taxes, militias, and courts. Great Britain handled the more far-reaching matters, such as regulating trade, managing American Indian and foreign affairs, and waging war. Governors and other crown-appointed officials acted as representatives of Great Britain. They enforced British law in the colonies and reported back to Parliament and the king.

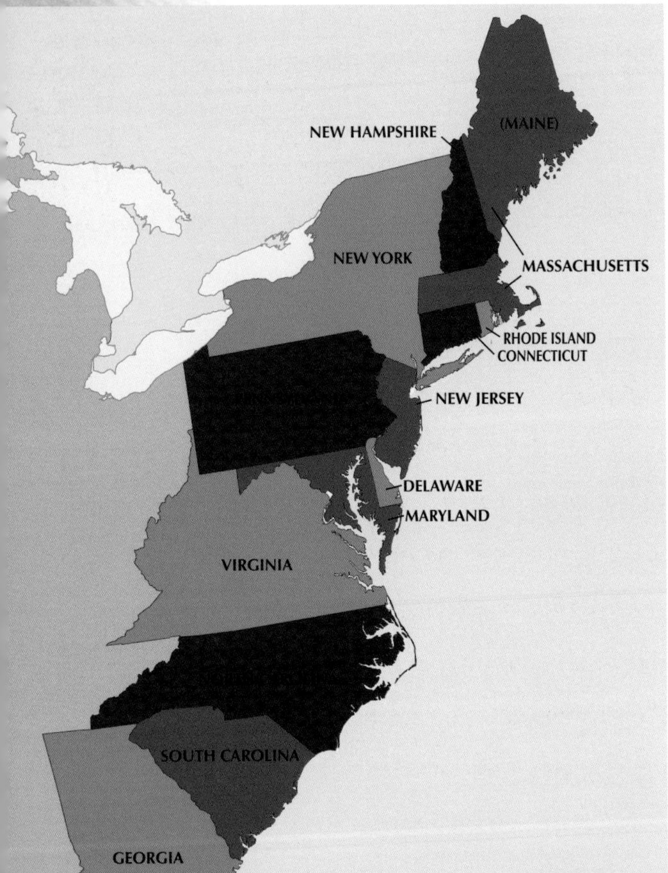

King George III was the leader of Great Britain, which included England, Scotland, and Wales. Although he was technically in charge, he did not control political policies and strategies. That required the input and agreement of government ministers and Parliament. Members of Parliament were elected by popular vote to represent British citizens in the national government.

Parliament's Stamp Act went into effect in the colonies in November 1765. It added a small tax to the cost of paper products such as deeds, mortgages, and newspapers. The income from the tax was to be used

NEW HAMPSHIRE (MAINE)

NEW YORK

MASSACHUSETTS

RHODE ISLAND
CONNECTICUT

NEW JERSEY

DELAWARE

MARYLAND

VIRGINIA

SOUTH CAROLINA

GEORGIA

N

All 13 American colonies were under British rule.

Colonists in Boston protested against the Stamp Act.

to fund a permanent force of 10,000 British troops in North America. Their job was to keep the peace between American Indians and the colonists.

The paper tax made perfect sense to the British government. The colonies needed to contribute money to their own defense. Colonists paid 25 times less in taxes than the British. In fact, the people of England had already gone through three stamp taxes with hardly any complaints.

But the colonies weren't England. The introduction of the Stamp Act in North America was met with outrage.

Many colonists claimed it was a violation of their rights. They pointed to British documents and customs that claimed Great Britain's subjects would not suffer taxation without representation. American colonists didn't have any representatives in Parliament, so they felt they should not have to pay the stamp tax.

The British public was puzzled by the colonists' fury. At the time the English weren't equally represented in Parliament. Most representatives came from small towns. The growing industrial centers weren't represented

A political cartoon features a horse, representing the colonies, bucking off a rider, representing Great Britain.

The colonists wanted the rights guaranteed to them, and they weren't willing to back down. They showed their displeasure by boycotting British goods, writing pamphlets, and harassing tax collectors. Some angrily vandalized and looted private property and businesses. The boycott severely damaged the British economy. It also upset British merchants who lost sales. A frustrated Parliament repealed the Stamp Act in March 1766.

The colonists' feelings of victory didn't last long. The Townshend Acts of 1767 introduced another set of taxes. This time products such as lead, tea, and paper imported from England were taxed.

Colonists protested and boycotted again. The Massachusetts legislature sent a letter to the other 12 colonies encouraging continent-wide resistance to the new law. Parliament demanded that Massachusetts recall the letter. The colony refused. Angered by the colony's

at all. Since the British didn't mind unequal representation, they didn't understand why it was a problem for the colonists.

disobedience, Parliament dissolved the Massachusetts government. The other colonies saw this as a threat to their own right to self-govern. All 12 joined the resistance.

The Townshend Acts were repealed in 1770 with the exception of the tax on British tea. By this point most colonists had stopped drinking tea. Those who did drink it bought Dutch tea from smugglers. Britain's East India Tea Company, which was already on the brink of financial disaster, needed income from the colonies to survive. Parliament tried to help the tea company with the passage of the Tea Act of 1773. This law reduced the cost of British tea in the colonies in the hope that the colonists would buy it.

The colonists, however, were furious. Even if they didn't personally buy the tea, they still had to pay the tax on it when it reached shore. They were once again being taxed without representation.

An anonymous group of Massachusetts men dressed roughly like American Indians quietly boarded three cargo ships in Boston Harbor on December 16, 1773. They politely requested the keys to the cargo area, located the chests of tea, and hacked into them with tomahawks. The 342 chests were tossed into the harbor.

The Boston Tea Party, as it came to be known, was an enormous insult to the British government. King George III wanted to take drastic action and show "the just dependence of the colonies upon the Crown and Parliament of Great Britain." Some in Parliament favored military action, but that would put the empire into more debt. Others wanted to punish the men who had

"We were surrounded by British armed ships, but no attempt was made to resist us."

—George Hewes, a participant in the Boston Tea Party

Colonists made their point to Parliament by dumping tea into Boston Harbor.

destroyed the tea, but their identities were unknown.

Prime Minister Lord North suggested punishing all Bostonians for treason even though most of them hadn't been involved in the tea party. He wanted to show the colonies that Great Britain would not tolerate their actions. Above all he wanted to demonstrate Parliament's right to govern the colonies and the colonists' duty to obey.

The Coercive Acts of 1774 were indeed harsh punishment. Boston's port was closed to trade, draining the local economy. Massachusetts' government was replaced with a Governor's Council appointed by the crown. Formal government meetings were restricted to one per year.

Only town officials were allowed to attend them.

The Coercive Acts, which the colonists called the Intolerable Acts, were meant to punish and humiliate the entire city. The anger felt in Boston spread to other American cities and colonies. For the first time, colonists who were loyal to the crown were questioning Great Britain's authority. They wanted the same rights allowed to British subjects on British soil.

The British government was also trying to uphold the rights of British subjects. The rights included protection. The government protected its citizens by maintaining its military forces. And that cost the government money. Money came from trade and taxes. Bowing to the colonists' demands would harm this process.

The British government wanted to protect its position of authority in the colonies too. That was worth keeping by any means necessary, including military force. Parliament highlighted that point in the summer of 1774 by moving 3,000 British troops into Boston.

ANNO DECIMO QUARTO

Georgii III. Regis.

C A P. XIX.

An Act to discontinue, in such Manner, and for such Time as are therein mentioned, the landing and discharging, lading or shipping, of Goods, Wares, and Merchandise, at the Town, and within the Harbour, of *Boston*, in the Province of *Massachuset's Bay*, in *North America.*

 WHEREAS dangerous Commotions and Insurrections have been fomented and raised in the Town of Boston, in the Province of Massachuset's Bay, in

The Boston Port Bill, one of the Coercive Acts, closed Boston's ports to trade.

CHAPTER TWO
EQUALITY
for All

Before 1774 most American colonists were proud to be part of the British Empire. Living under British rule meant naval protection and access to inexpensive manufactured goods. But the colonists' loyalty lay with King George III, not Parliament. In their eyes it was Parliament, not the king, that was passing restrictive laws such as the Coercive Acts. Many colonists feared that Parliament was trying to enslave the colonies.

Bostonians protested the Coercive Acts by boycotting British goods. Trade was an important part of the relationship between Great Britain and the colonies. With no manufacturing capabilities of their own, each American settlement needed goods imported from England. In turn, Great Britain's economy relied on the money brought in by trade with the colonies. The Coercive Acts were crippling Boston's economy. To the colonists, it seemed only fair to return the favor. They hoped their boycott would hurt the British economy.

Newspapers spread the word of the boycott to the rest of Massachusetts and beyond. Sympathy for Bostonians grew. Little by little, resistance against the Coercive Acts sprang up throughout

Colonists feed caged Bostonians who are surrounded by British military forces in a 1774 political cartoon.

the Northeast. The colonists supporting resistance against the British were called patriots.

But not everyone felt the need for resistance. Some colonists still supported Parliament. Known as loyalists, they believed the colonies needed Great Britain for survival. Many felt that Great Britain was within its rights to tax its American subjects. Some loyalists, however, opposed both Parliament's laws and the radical behavior exhibited by the patriots. When forced to take sides, they chose Great Britain. Some loyalists suffered at the hands of their patriot neighbors. They were jeered at, beaten, and even tarred and feathered. Crown-appointed officials serving in the areas surrounding Boston were harassed and eventually chased out of town.

Across the Atlantic Ocean, King George III and Parliament weren't worried. They figured that only working-class city dwellers and local clergy were upset. They thought average citizens would turn their backs on the troublemakers. They had no idea that the rebellion was taking over the countryside.

Colonial leaders decided to meet to discuss the problems they were facing. The First Continental Congress met on September 5, 1774, in Philadelphia, Pennsylvania. Every colony except Georgia sent representatives. They wanted to respond to the Coercive Acts.

Independence was not a major topic of conversation at the First Continental Congress. Very few members were in favor of separating from Great Britain. Instead, the group focused on how to acquire the liberties given to other subjects of the British crown. Their final product was a Declaration of Rights and Grievances.

◀ Patriots forced loyalists out of town.

It defined the rights of Americans. It also set limits on Parliament's power.

The document noted that the colonists who originally settled North America in the 1600s were allowed the same rights they had enjoyed in England. Therefore, the people who lived in North America now should also enjoy those rights. The document also said everyone had the right to gather freely and participate in government. Since the colonists were not represented in Parliament, they should be free to form their own legislative bodies in the colonies. The legislative bodies should be responsible for enacting taxes and other legislation. Parliament should only control trade.

The Congress also drafted the Continental Association. It was a boycott of trade with Great Britain until the Coercive Acts were repealed.

The First Continental Congress was held at Carpenters' Hall in Philadelphia, Pennsylvania.

The task of enforcing the boycott went to the people. Local committees made sure colonists followed the new trading rules. Those who violated the Association were called out in public and left out of future business dealings.

The committees soon expanded their power beyond matters of trade.

◄ The First Continental Congress hoped to unite the colonies in their resistance to the Coercive Acts.

They ensured that newspapers printed articles only in favor of the rebellion. They also forced colonists to choose sides by signing loyalty oaths. Those who would not sign were assumed to be supporters of Parliament. Sometimes loyalists were still allowed to live in town, but nobody would talk to them.

News of the Declaration of Rights and Grievances and the Association arrived in London in December 1774. Members of Parliament were conflicted about how to respond. Some wanted to use force. The British believed that the colonists would be easy to beat. They had no real standing army and no navy at all. But the colonies were spread out over a large swath of land. It would be hard for Great Britain to defend all of it. And what would happen if the Americans could gather an effective army?

> **"[The British constitution] with all its imperfections is, and ever will be, the pride and envy of mankind."**
>
> —James Chalmers, a loyalist

King George III didn't share those worries. He was ready to go to war. He said that "blows must decide" whether Americans "submit or triumph." After six weeks of debate, members of Parliament eventually agreed. They realized that backing down now would mean losing control of the colonies forever.

The colonists didn't want to fight the British Army, but their protests were being ignored. Taking arms against Great Britain was the only form of resistance they hadn't tried. In the spring of 1775, colonists readied their hunting rifles. They prepared to defend both their rights and their homes.

They didn't have to wait long. Seven hundred members of the British Army arrived in Lexington, Massachusetts, on April 19, 1775. The Redcoats, nicknamed for their brightly colored

LIEUTENANT GENERAL THOMAS GAGE

Lieutenant General Thomas Gage became commander of British forces in North America after the French and Indian War. He was alarmed by what he saw happening in the colonies. The colonists became more and more aggressive with the passing of each new act. Loyalists and British representatives were attacked. Gage shared his concerns with British officials during a trip back to England in 1773. The Coercive Acts were passed soon thereafter.

Gage was named governor of Massachusetts in 1774. His primary duty was to enforce the Coercive Acts. He removed colonial judges, appointed crown representatives, and eliminated town meetings. He also earned the scorn of angry colonists. There was no doubt in Gage's mind that the colonists were ready to fight. Gage sent reports to England detailing the increasing violence in the colonies. He cautioned that the rebellion was much larger and stronger than they understood. Parliament thought he was exaggerating.

Gage remained in the colonies during the early part of the war. He returned to Great Britain in October 1775 and advised military leaders from there.

Minutemen and Redcoats battled in Lexington.

uniforms, came to arrest patriots John Hancock and Samuel Adams for acts of rebellion. Then they would march to nearby Concord to seize colonial military supplies. Hancock and Adams were long gone. They had escaped to a nearby town after being warned of the Redcoats' approach. Paul Revere, a local silversmith, and William Dawes, a tanner, brought the news as they rode their horses through the countryside to warn local militias that the British Army was boarding boats in the Charles River. When the Redcoats finally arrived in Lexington, they were greeted by about 100 colonial Minutemen.

The Minutemen were part of the Massachusetts militia. They were its youngest members, named for their ability to be ready "at a minute's notice." In the past the militia mainly defended colonial property from

American Indians. Now its members were ready to fight the country that had protected them for so long.

The Minutemen in Lexington were greatly outnumbered. They were ordered to put down their weapons. Some of them did. Others held their rifles tightly. Nobody knows which side shot first, but that one gunshot spurred both sides into action. Within minutes 10 militia members were dead. Nine more were injured.

The British continued marching toward Concord. Lieutenant General Thomas Gage wanted to make sure that the rebels didn't have any weapons or ammunition with which to fight. But when his men arrived in Concord, they were able to find only a cannon, some musket balls, and sacks of flour.

As the British searched the area surrounding Concord, they encountered 1,000 militia soldiers who had gathered during the search for weapons. British commanders called for backup, but the additional 1,100 soldiers who arrived couldn't hold off the colonists. The British were just trying to get back home. The colonists were looking for blood. At the end of the first day of battle, about 270 British soldiers had been killed or wounded. Fewer than 100 Americans met the same fate. Great Britain and the colonies were now at war.

British troops were ambushed by the militia in Concord.

CHAPTER THREE

LOYALTY
Is Tested

News of the battle spread like wildfire through the northeastern colonies. The British retreated to Boston, but that didn't stop the patriots. Hundreds of men from all over Massachusetts continued to arrive for a full day after the retreat and formed a human wall around the city.

The mobilization of militias wasn't limited to Massachusetts. Connecticut quickly ordered 6,000 men to join the patriot troops surrounding Boston. Other colonies followed suit. Within a week more than 16,000 men from four northeastern colonies surrounded the British Army in Boston.

Lieutenant General Gage and his men had been put in control of Boston in 1774. Now they were also trapped there. At the time of the revolution, Boston was essentially an island. Only a small strip of land connected the city to the mainland. It was fairly easy for the patriots to keep the British confined. Gage made no effort to break free.

King George III was ready to deal a severe blow to the colonies. "America must be a colony of England or treated as an enemy," he vowed. To the king, having colonies with an equal voice in the government was worse than not having the colonies in the empire.

The local militias around Boston would eventually become the first soldiers in the Continental Army.

Some British people felt that the colonies were worth holding onto even if it meant compromising. The colonies were an important source of raw materials, such as lumber and tobacco. They also poured a lot of money into the British economy through trade. Many British citizens feared the loss of the colonies. They worried about what would happen if the colonies separated from the British Empire.

Back in North America, the rebels were proud of their achievements. They weren't a traditional army with first-class training, but they believed they had the determination and bravery needed to defeat the British. Now that the war had started, many patriot leaders realized that there was no turning back. The soldiers were ready to fight. A war had begun. How to handle that war was the focus of the Second Continental Congress, which gathered in Philadelphia on May 10, 1775.

Congress was never meant to be a governing body. It was supposed to be a forum for exchanging ideas about how each colony could most effectively protest British policies. But now this new union needed leaders. The Second Continental Congress appointed itself the central government for the American colonies. Its first task was to decide how to handle the dozens of local militias surrounding Boston. Congress knew that a real army—one that trained its men—was necessary. It established the Continental Army, the first independent army in American history. Led by George Washington, its first members were patriot militias stationed outside Boston.

Even though all signs pointed to war, the Continental Congress wanted to make it clear that the colonies were still loyal to Great Britain. Any action on the battlefield was to protect the colonies from the policies of the king's ministers. They still blamed Parliament,

GEORGE WASHINGTON

George Washington didn't intend to lead the Continental Army. He retired from the Virginia militia after the French and Indian War, intent on becoming a farmer. That changed with the passing of the Coercive Acts. He became a vocal opponent of the new laws, which led to his appointment to both sessions of the Continental Congress.

Despite his military experience, Washington felt he wasn't qualified to lead the Continental Army. Some congressmen agreed. But they also agreed that Washington's most outstanding quality was a political one. As a Virginian, Washington had the support of Virginia—the largest and wealthiest colony. Virginia's resources would help strengthen the Continental Army. Support from Virginia was important. Washington eventually accepted the position out of duty. His service did not end after the war. Washington was elected the first president of the United States in 1789.

not the king. They thought that as soon as King George III gained control of his advisers, the fighting would come to an end. Congress outlined this in the Olive Branch Petition, which was sent to England on July 8, 1775. It would take at least two and a half months for the document to travel across the Atlantic Ocean. Congress eagerly awaited the king's response.

The patriots surrounding Boston were also waiting. Lieutenant General Gage's men had been holed up inside the city for two months. Activity was limited to British reinforcements and supplies arriving in the harbor. But the stream of shipments paid off. Gage had 8,000 men in Boston by June 1775. The British were finally ready to break free from the city and crush the rebels once and for all.

"I declare it before God, the congregation, and all the world, … that it is not a rebellion to oppose any King, Ministry, or Governor, that destroys by any violence or authority whatever, the Rights of the People."

—The Reverend John Allen of Boston

The Americans heard about the forthcoming attack and readied themselves for battle. It came on June 17, when 2,500 British soldiers clashed with 1,200 patriots on top of Breed's Hill in Boston. The Battle of Bunker Hill (named for the nearby hill the British initially planned to attack) was short yet bloody. Technically it was a victory for the British. The Americans had to retreat after they ran out of ammunition. But based on casualties, the Continental Army came out on top. Deaths and injuries numbered 1,000 for the British. The Americans lost fewer than 500. Both parties retreated to their starting places and waited for the next opportunity to attack.

King George III learned about the devastating losses at Breed's Hill on the

At the Battle of Bunker Hill, the colonists lost fewer men than the British but had to retreat when they ran out of ammunition.

same day he received Congress's Olive Branch Petition. He refused to look at the petition. Instead, he officially declared the colonies to be in a state of rebellion.

But not all of the colonists were rebelling against Great Britain. About 20 percent of Americans were still loyal to the crown. Loyalists were often upper-class landowners or clergy from the Church of England. Landowners and civil servants felt a debt to the crown for their possessions and positions.

Patriots were generally middle class: lawyers, merchants, and planters. They, however, were the leaders of the rebellion, not the actual fighters. Fighting was left to the lower-class farmers and laborers. Politically, the

Farmers and laborers did most of the fighting during the Revolutionary War.

lower class didn't have much loyalty to either side. Many depended on upper-class landowners for their livelihoods. Some of the men fought for a small compensation of money or land after their service was over. Some were inspired to fight by the rebellion's middle-class leaders.

In the 1770s 25 percent of the people living in the colonies were enslaved. They, too, had no real loyalty to either side. Their primary concern was not equality with other British subjects but their own personal freedom. Lord Dunmore, royal governor of Virginia, latched onto that idea in November 1775. He offered freedom to any slave of a Virginia patriot master if the slave joined the British Army. Eight hundred men answered the call, outraging slave owners. The rebels made no similar offer. By the spring of 1775 African-Americans weren't allowed to serve in the Continental Army, despite the fact that many had fought at Lexington and Concord.

By the end of 1775, most of the crown-appointed governors in the colonies had escaped to the safety of British warships. The only place Great Britain controlled was Boston, which remained under siege. Yet independence from Great Britain was hardly mentioned.

That changed with the passing of the new year. Patriot Thomas Paine published a pamphlet in January 1776 that railed against the tyranny of the British monarchy. Called *Common Sense*, the pamphlet argued that the British government was abusing its power over the American colonies. The only option was to declare independence from Great Britain. Paine's ideas weren't new, but they were presented in a way that the average person could understand. For the first time in history, the American colonists seriously began to consider independence from Great Britain.

COMMON SENSE;

ADDRESSED TO THE

INHABITANTS

OF

AMERICA,

On the following interesting

SUBJECTS.

I. Of the Origin and Design of Government in general, with concise Remarks on the English Constitution.

II. Of Monarchy and Hereditary Succession.

III. Thoughts on the present State of American Affairs.

IV. Of the present Ability of America, with some miscellaneous Reflections.

After *Common Sense* was published, more colonists supported independence.

CHAPTER FOUR

FIGHTING
for Freedom

Chatter of independence filled taverns and town halls at the beginning of 1776 as General Washington prepared for one final push against the Redcoats. In early March cannons were positioned on Dorchester Heights in Boston, overlooking the city and its port. The Continental Army bombarded the city and harbor with cannon fire. General William Howe, who had replaced General Gage as commander of the British Army, retreated on March 17 with 11,000 British troops and 1,000 loyalists. They sailed to Halifax, Nova Scotia, a Canadian colony of the crown.

Washington suspected that the British would head for New York City next. In preparation, he moved about 18,000 patriot soldiers to Brooklyn Heights, Governors Island, and lower Manhattan.

Washington's instincts were right. General Howe arrived on Staten Island on July 2. An army of 32,000 men trickled in over the next month and a half. It was the largest force Great Britain had ever sent overseas. Great Britain had a military that traveled wherever they were needed. For these soldiers, the military was a lifelong occupation. They were only discharged when they were considered

George Washington's troops traveled to New York City to defend the area from the British Army.

no longer able to serve. In addition to the Redcoats and loyalist soldiers, Howe's army included 8,000 German mercenaries known as Hessians. German states rented out soldiers to the highest bidders. Most of the rented soldiers came from Hesse-Kassel, hence their name. The Hessians fought for money, not politics. But most of the money they earned went to their rulers. By the end of the war, Great Britain would employ 30,000 Hessian fighters.

For some Americans, the Hessian soldiers were the tipping point for supporting the movement for independence. The Prohibitory Act convinced thousands of others. Passed at the end of 1775, the act allowed the British Navy to stop American ships at sea and seize the goods on board. Patriot sailors could even be forced to join the Royal Navy. The colonists were furious. The colonies relied heavily on imports and exports for goods and income.

The Continental Congress was also thinking hard about independence. The American colonies didn't have enough money or arms to fight a full-on war. They needed outside help. The most likely candidates were France and Spain. France had lost almost all of its American territory to Great Britain during the French and Indian War. What it didn't lose was given to Spain, which now controlled land west of the Mississippi River. France wanted revenge on Great Britain for having taken the land. The country also thought that if the colonies separated from Great Britain, it would make their enemy less powerful. Colonial leaders knew that France and Spain would only join the revolution if the colonies officially separated themselves from Great Britain.

Congressman Richard Henry Lee of Virginia introduced a resolution on June 7, 1776, that declared the independence of the colonies from

Great Britain. Delegates from Delaware, New Jersey, and Pennsylvania required convincing, but on July 2, Congress unanimously voted in favor of independence. Ties with Great Britain were officially severed.

The Declaration of Independence was approved by Congress on July 4, 1776. It explained why independence was necessary. It listed the colonies' grievances with King George III and Parliament. It told how the British government was unwilling to compromise.

The British government tried to ignore the declaration. It was called a meaningless document written by unhappy people. While some people in Great Britain supported American independence, most were alarmed. Many wondered if the American government could be trusted, since it was founded by a rebellion. Of even more concern was the money the colonies had borrowed from British lenders prior to the revolution. People wondered if that money would ever be repaid.

In the summer of 1776, the Continental Army began fighting for independence. But every battle was

General William Howe commanded British forces in the colonies.

a bloody defeat. Fighting began on August 22 in Brooklyn, New York. Howe and 20,000 of his men showed just how deadly a professional army could be, crushing the patriots on August 29. With victory after victory, the British forced the rebel army out of New York, through New Jersey, and into Pennsylvania.

	BRITISH ARMED FORCES	CONTINENTAL ARMY
SIZE	42,000 professional soldiers 30,000 Hessian soldiers 20,000 loyalists	20,000 soldiers
LENGTH OF COMMITMENT	for life	3 years
TRAINING	excellent	poor
EXPERIENCE	very little	none
MILITARY DISCIPLINE	excellent	poor
PAYMENT	8 pence/day (about $4.50 today)	$20 signing bonus (about $600 today) 100 acres of land after discharge

The Continental Army and British forces did not have equal numbers, experience, or compensation.

By December the Continental Army was a ragged mess. It had lost 5,000 men to injury, death, or capture since fighting had begun in August. Now it had fewer than 3,000 men, who were hungry, barely clothed, and in desperate need of weapons and supplies. Howe didn't think it was necessary to chase an army that was so close to destruction. He and his men settled down in New Jersey to wait for spring.

Washington wasn't ready to give up. He led a surprise attack on 1,200 Hessian soldiers on December 26, 1776, in Trenton. Nine hundred were taken prisoner. He struck again on January 3, 1777, defeating three British regiments at Princeton. The British retreated to their headquarters in New York. The Americans now controlled New Jersey.

The spirits of the Continental troops were boosted by their winter victories. At that time Continental soldiers served for only one year. Washington decided he needed a long-term army. Congress agreed. In early 1777 it offered a $20 signing bonus and 100 acres (40.5 hectares) of land in exchange for three years of service in the Continental Army. Free African-Americans and slaves were allowed to serve as well. Should numbers fall short, the colonies could draft men for service.

Great Britain was also recruiting additional forces. Both Americans and the British had been vying for support from the Iroquois Confederacy since the beginning of the war. Made up of six tribes, it was the most powerful native nation in the North. At first the Iroquois resisted invitations of alliance. But they soon realized that whoever won the war would decide the fate of the native people too. Four of the six tribes felt they had a better chance of keeping their homelands if Great Britain won the war. They joined the

Chief Joseph Brant was a Mohawk leader who supported the British during the war.

Redcoats after the Battle of Long Island in 1776. The other two Iroquois tribes joined the patriots.

Armed with Iroquois fighters, Great Britain unveiled a complicated plan for 1777. Three British officers—

General John Burgoyne, Barry St. Leger, and Howe—would start their troops at opposite edges of New York and meet in the city of Albany, leaving a path of destruction in their wake. It would separate the more rebellious northeastern colonies from the southern colonies, which the British felt they still had a chance to reclaim.

The plan worked better on paper than in practice. Burgoyne and his army of 7,000 British soldiers and 1,000 Iroquois began their march from Montreal, Canada, at the end of June 1777. They arrived in Albany in the middle of July. But Howe and St. Leger never arrived. St. Leger was held up at the edge of Lake Ontario. Howe had decided to go to Philadelphia instead. Burgoyne and his men were on their own.

They crossed the Hudson River on September 13, 1777, and were met by the Continental Army near Saratoga, New York. The British were soundly defeated over the course of the next month. Burgoyne was left with only 5,000 men at his command. He surrendered on October 17. Howe fared better in Philadelphia. His regiment defeated Washington in October. The Americans retreated to nearby Valley Forge for the winter.

During the six months at Valley Forge, 2,500 out of Washington's 10,000 soldiers died from starvation, malnutrition, or the bitter cold. The British were able to pay local farmers more for food supplies, making food scarce for Washington's army. Many soldiers may have considered deserting their comrades. But Washington had warned that any deserters would be shot on sight. By spring though, supply lines had been reopened. The Americans finally had shoes, blankets, and food.

Near the end of winter, Prussian General Baron Friedrich Wilhelm von Steuben joined the Americans at

Colonial troops spent a miserable winter at Valley Forge.

Valley Forge. He had become friendly with Benjamin Franklin, who was representing the colonies in Paris. Franklin knew the Continental Army was in need of help. Von Steuben seemed to be just the man. He created a strict training program for the Americans. They learned how to march, use bayonets, and follow orders. The colonists emerged from Valley Forge in June 1778 ready to fight alongside their new allies: the French.

CHAPTER FIVE
WAR
Turns Global

The French wanted revenge on the British for the French and Indian War. Great Britain's victory meant that France lost its presence in North America. Before the French and Indian War, England controlled only the 13 American colonies and Nova Scotia. Spain had Florida and Mexico. France owned Louisiana, which at the time included everything between the Mississippi Valley and the Appalachian Mountains, from the Gulf of Mexico to the northeastern part of Canada. After the war France's Canadian territories and the eastern part of Louisiana were ceded to the British.

France gave Spain everything west of the Mississippi River in an effort to keep it out of British control. So Great Britain wasn't surprised that the French government supported the patriots. At first the French secretly sent money and supplies to help the enemy of their enemy. France didn't want to declare the alliance publicly until it looked as if the Americans had a good shot at beating the British.

The American victory at Saratoga was the proof the French needed. Representatives from France and the American colonies signed two treaties on February 6, 1778. The Treaty of

The first French troops, led by the Count de Rochambeau (left), met with George Washington in 1780.

Benjamin Franklin (center) negotiated treaties with French officials.

Alliance said a peace negotiation with Great Britain required the approval of both France and the American colonies. It also said that any peace agreements had to include American independence. The Treaty of Amity and Commerce promoted trade between the two countries. The Continental Army now had more money and more military might.

The French fleet sailed for North America in April 1778. Twelve battleships arrived near Philadelphia on July 8, but the British soldiers occupying the city had already fled to New York for safety. They were accompanied by hundreds of American loyalists. Finding the city empty, the French immediately turned around and headed toward New Jersey. The French chased the British ships up the eastern shore but never landed to engage in battle. The fleet left in November to support the French invasion of the British West Indies. France was an American ally, but its

> "It is a common observation [in Paris] that our cause is the cause of all mankind, and that we are fighting for their liberty in defending our own."
>
> —Benjamin Franklin, in a letter to his friend Samuel Cooper, 1777

the cave and keeping of
your.

Kayms sleepover.

two can keep a secret

Can you smile?

primary goal was to take British land and protect its own.

Great Britain's American Indian allies had that same goal. More than a decade earlier, the Proclamation of 1763 said that all land west of the Appalachian Mountains was for American Indians, not colonists. Virginia governor Lord Dunmore violated that rule in 1774 when he tried to claim land outside of the Virginia settlement. A war between the colonists and the Delaware and Shawnee tribes followed. It was clear that the colonists would continue trying to expand their territory. American Indians who sided with the British did so in hopes of maintaining what little land they had.

Most Americans thought all the American Indians supported the monarchy. But in reality, the tribes were looking out for themselves. Several American Indian tribes supported their colonial neighbors.

BENJAMIN FRANKLIN

Benjamin Franklin spent the majority of the revolution in Europe. He was an envoy, representing the American government in its dealings with other governments. Franklin was sent to France after the Continental Congress declared independence in 1776. His mission was to negotiate an alliance. He also led an intelligence agency so he could keep General Washington informed about what was happening in both Great Britain and France.

Franklin made an impact on the French public. They admired his honesty and simple nature, which he exaggerated for their benefit. Anything having to do with Franklin or the American colonies became all the rage in Paris. It helped convince the French government that an alliance with the colonies was a good idea.

After the war Franklin returned to the United States. He was elected the Pennsylvania representative for the Constitutional Convention, which created a revised U.S. Constitution. Franklin remained involved in politics, science, and education throughout his life.

Some responded to the call from colonial missionaries who had been involved in their tribes. Some volunteered as Minutemen.

King George III and his advisers decided they had no chance of winning back the northern colonies after France joined the war. Yet they thought they might still be able to conquer the South. The British believed southerners were more loyal to the crown. The British thought these southerners would be happy to take up arms for Great Britain. And combining them with American Indian volunteers meant there would be very little need for additional British forces. But in truth, only about 16 percent of Americans in the South were loyalists. As in the North, a bitter civil war between patriots and loyalists had been brewing for a year. By 1776 the patriots had taken control of all government in Georgia, South Carolina, North Carolina, and Virginia. The king's advisers in the colonies had fled to the safety of British warships. Wanting to avoid looking foolish, many never mentioned any of this in their reports to the crown.

Still, the South was Great Britain's safest bet for winning back at least part of the colonies. British general Sir

Logan, a leader of the Mingo tribe, fought colonists after a colonial trader murdered his entire family.

Henry Clinton used the Royal Navy to transport his men from New York to Georgia. He attacked Savannah on December 29, 1778, with 3,500 British soldiers and 1,000 local loyalists. Their capture of the city ignited battles throughout Georgia and the Carolinas.

Help was on the way for the colonies. Spain declared war against Great Britain on June 21, 1779. It was in Spain's best interest to support the colonies. Spanish Louisiana, which covered land west of the Mississippi River from the Gulf of Mexico to the Canadian border, was the only thing standing in the way of British westward expansion. If the colonies gained independence, Spain wouldn't have to worry about Britain expanding its territory in North America. Spain's alliance with the Americans was bad news for the British. Not only were their enemies getting more help, but what had started as an attempt to control the American colonies was turning into a major European war.

France and Spain began attacking the British fortress at Gibraltar on June 24, 1779. Gibraltar was the gateway between the Atlantic Ocean and the Mediterranean Sea. Whoever controlled it controlled trade between the Mediterranean and the rest of the world. Gibraltar belonged to Great Britain, and the empire couldn't afford to lose it. The British were forced to divert some of their forces in the colonies to the Mediterranean to respond to the attack.

It was just the beginning of international warfare. Soon the British were fighting to hold on to territories in the West Indies, the Mediterranean, Africa, and India. Troops were spread thin, and costs were mounting. It wouldn't be long before the people footing the bill had something to say about it.

CHAPTER SIX
REBELS
Gain Ground

War is expensive. By 1780 the newly created American government was almost bankrupt. It had $30 million in reserves—silver and gold that backed the value of printed money. But the government had printed $400 million in paper money. Forty dollars in paper was worth only $1 in silver. Prices of goods skyrocketed. American troops weren't being paid. They threatened to revolt.

With 180,000 men volunteering for military service, women were in charge of running the households, family businesses, and farms. It wasn't easy. Armies from both sides confiscated farmland for food and campgrounds. Many of the slaves who worked in homes or on farms escaped to join the British or Continental armies. The war was draining the colonies of their resources and workforce.

Loyalist families had it particularly hard. Angry patriots attacked families publicly loyal to the crown. They lost everything, including their homes. Many loyalists had fled to Spanish Florida or British-occupied New York by 1780. Thousands more were homeless and penniless. They hid in forests and swamps, waiting for rescue by the British Army.

The legend of Molly Pitcher tells the story of an unknown colonial woman who took over her husband's cannon when he was killed in battle.

Great Britain is represented as an old man desperately trying to hold on to the colonies in a 1777 political cartoon.

Times were tough in Great Britain too. The empire's debt had almost doubled. The colonists weren't paying any British taxes at all, so it was up to the British public to fund the war. Taxes were at an all-time high. Slowly but surely, more British citizens spoke out against the war and the toll it was taking on the British economy.

That was exactly what American leaders wanted. To win the war, they didn't have to destroy the British Army. They only had to keep the rebellion going until the British taxpayers demanded an end to the war.

As British public opinion turned against the war, so did the opinion of previously neutral nations. Countries all over the world were angry about Great Britain's Prohibitory Act. In addition to boarding and seizing American ships, the British could confiscate any supplies suspected of going to the colonies. Nations that had not yet taken a side in the war were losing money on late shipments and confiscated goods. Great Britain was on the verge of making more enemies in Europe and beyond.

Catherine the Great, the empress of Russia, had seen enough by March 1780. She issued a Declaration of Armed Neutrality. It said that neutral ships were free to transport any legal goods, including those belonging to warring nations. Denmark and Sweden joined Russia by the end of the summer, forming the League of Armed Neutrality. For the most part, Great Britain followed the rules, cautious of angering any other heads of state. Neutral ships freely went back and forth between Europe and North America, bringing supplies and hope to the colonists.

Colonists were desperate for both. Great Britain's southern strategy was working. In the span of 20 months, the British demolished three American armies; captured Savannah, Georgia, and Charleston, South Carolina; and occupied a large part of rural South Carolina. More than 7,000 Continental soldiers were wounded or killed, equaling the British losses at Saratoga.

Catherine the Great, Russian empress

But the mood in the South was changing. Instead of submitting to British occupation, patriots and loyalists alike began to regard the British with suspicion. This was due to a set of decrees issued after the capture of Charleston on May 12, 1780. All southern patriots who had been paroled from prison were forced to take an oath of allegiance to the crown. Then the prisoners had to join the loyalist militia and fight against their former comrades. Those who didn't take the oath would be put back in jail and have their property taken away.

Some paroled patriots fled to the countryside. Others took the oath without intending to obey it. They benefitted from the crown's protection while still secretly fighting for independence. True loyalists were disgusted by the false oaths of allegiance. Many left the area or became neutral. Some joined the patriot cause.

Some patriots tried to reclaim their land from the British on their own. Independent militias emerged from the swamps and forests to ambush British patrol units and supply trains. South Carolina was back in a state of rebellion by September. In October a patriot militia slaughtered a British-led loyalist army of 1,000 men at Kings Mountain in North Carolina. After that it was nearly impossible to persuade loyalists to fight for Great Britain.

The British troops had to continue without loyalist military support. British general Charles Cornwallis took an army of 4,000 to the Carolinas in January 1781 with hopes of cutting rebel supply routes. The Redcoats were soundly defeated at the Cowpens, a large field in South Carolina. They also suffered enormous losses during a battle in front of the Guilford Courthouse in March. Over the course of the two battles, the British suffered a loss of 1,700 men injured, captured,

The Battle of Cowpens was a turning point for the Continental Army fighting in the South.

or killed. That was 40 percent of the regiment. The Continental Army and local patriot militias had a total of only 337 casualties. Many of the wounded Americans came back to fight a few weeks later.

General Cornwallis attempted to cut supply routes again in April. This time he took his men away from the rebel-controlled Carolinas and into Virginia. Instead of simply blocking supply lines between Virginia and South Carolina, British troops destroyed them. Barns filled with animal feed were burned to the ground. Young horses were killed before they could be moved to the front lines with the American cavalry. For three months the British harassed citizens, destroyed property, and took over farms. Anything that could help the patriots was considered to be fair game. But Cornwallis's plan backfired. Virginians, who had previously been mostly untouched by the war, reacted angrily. Patriot militias grew. More Virginians enlisted in the Continental Army.

The British eventually retreated to Yorktown, Virginia. Yorktown was part of a narrow peninsula that jutted into the Atlantic Ocean. It had good access to waterways but very few escape routes by land. The Americans took advantage of that. Washington and 17,000 men from the Continental and French armies and local patriot militias attacked on September 28. The battle raged for three weeks. The 9,000 British soldiers were grossly outnumbered.

On October 19, 1781, the British surrendered. There was nothing worse for Great Britain's professional army than to admit defeat at the hands of the inexperienced Americans. Even admitting defeat to the French was more acceptable, and General Cornwallis's second in command tried to surrender to the French to avoid having to surrender to the Americans. But the French commander declined the surrender, forcing the British to deal directly with General Washington.

It took more than a month for the news of surrender to reach King George III and Parliament. It was a dreadful surprise. For months the king and his advisers had known that the battle at Yorktown would decide the outcome of the war. But King George III refused to acknowledge defeat. He vowed that the war would continue.

The British surrendered to the Continental Army after the Battle of Yorktown. ▶

CHAPTER SEVEN
TREATY
of Paris

Despite King George III's protests, the Battle of Yorktown was the last major battle in the colonies. The 26,000 British troops remaining in North America were in British-controlled New York, Charleston and Savannah in the South, and around the Great Lakes and Lake Champlain in Canada. The Royal Navy patrolled the Atlantic coast. But the lack of public support and an army spread across the world meant that, with the exception of a few minor skirmishes in the south and west, there wouldn't be any more fighting in North America. The war was finally coming to an end.

Formal peace negotiations between the American colonies and Great Britain began on September 27, 1782, two months after the British evacuated Savannah. Benjamin Franklin was in charge of negotiating for the Americans. His first priority was for Great Britain to formally recognize American independence. He also wanted Great Britain to give Canada to the colonies. Great Britain was unprepared for that request. It took two more months of discussion and bargaining before the articles of peace between the two nations were signed on November 30, 1782.

A GENERAL PEACE

NEW-YORK, March 25, 1783

LATE laſt Night, an EXPRESS from New-Jerſey, brought the following Account.

THAT on Sunday laſt, the Twenty-Third Inſtant, a Veſſel arrived at Philadelphia, in Thirty-five Days from Cadiz, with *Diſpatches* to the *Continental Congreſs*, informing them, that on Monday the Twentieth Day of January, the PRELIMINARIES to

A GENERAL PEACE,

Between *Great-Britain, France, Spain, Holland,* and the *United States of America,* were SIGNED at Paris, by all the Commiſſioners from thoſe Powers, in conſequence of which, Hoſtilities, by Sea and Land, were to *ceaſe* in Europe, on Wedneſday the Twentieth Day of February ; and in America, on Thurſday the Twentieth Day of March, in the preſent Year One Thouſand Seven Hundred and Eighty-Three.

THIS very *important* Intelligence was laſt Night announced by the Firing of Cannon, and great Rejoicings at Elizabeth-Town.---Reſpecting the Particulars of this truly intereſting Event no more are yet received, but they are hourly expected.

A peace announcement was distributed in New York.

Under the terms of the agreement, Great Britain formally recognized American independence. All territory east of the Mississippi River was under American control. Canada remained under the control of Great Britain, but American fishermen were allowed access to certain Canadian fishing areas. In return, the Americans promised to pay back prewar British loans and restore the property lost by loyalists during the war. The agreement also allowed for the evacuation of British troops from the colonies.

Great Britain negotiated similar treaties with France and Spain. The formal Treaty of Paris was signed on September 3, 1783. The last British troops in the colonies left New York on November 25.

The American Revolutionary War resulted in thousands of deaths and the destruction of property. After all of that, did the warring nations achieve their goals for going to war? The nations that entered the war last had the least to show for it. The League of Armed Neutrality, which eventually included Russia, Prussia, Austria, Sweden, Denmark, the Dutch United Provinces, and Portugal, didn't see much change

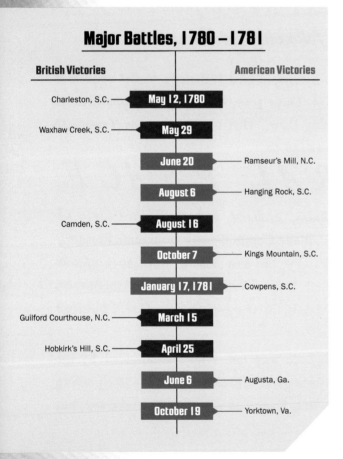

Major Battles, 1780 – 1781

British Victories		American Victories
Charleston, S.C.	May 12, 1780	
Waxhaw Creek, S.C.	May 29	
	June 20	Ramseur's Mill, N.C.
	August 6	Hanging Rock, S.C.
Camden, S.C.	August 16	
	October 7	Kings Mountain, S.C.
	January 17, 1781	Cowpens, S.C.
Guilford Courthouse, N.C.	March 15	
Hobkirk's Hill, S.C.	April 25	
	June 6	Augusta, Ga.
	October 19	Yorktown, Va.

In the last two years of the war, both sides saw wins and losses.

in the way Great Britain approached neutral ships. When neutral ships were able to reach American shores, it was more likely because the Royal Navy was too busy with other assignments. But the league did manage to threaten Great Britain's power in Europe, which turned British resources away from the war in North America.

Spain's entry into the war also decreased the amount of British resources available for battle against the colonists. Spain's goal was simple: maintain control of its property in North America. That goal was achieved—land west of the Mississippi River belonged to Spain. Spain also received the parts of Florida it didn't control before the war.

Revenge was the main reason why France fought in the Revolutionary War. The powerful European nation was humiliated after its defeat in the French and Indian War. Did the French get the revenge they so desired?

That's debatable. France gained no major territories during the war, nor did it replace Great Britain as a major European power. In fact, the American Revolution left France facing a financial disaster. It would eventually lead to the French Revolution in 1789.

Great Britain's allies didn't fare much better. The American Indians who fought alongside the British had joined the war to protect their own lands. But the British ceded everything east of the Mississippi River to the Americans, even though many tribes had long ago laid claim to those areas.

Americans loyal to the crown also suffered. They wanted Great Britain to continue ruling the colonies. Instead they were jeered at and attacked by their patriot neighbors. Many lost every penny they had. By the end of 1783, more than 100,000 loyalists had fled the colonies for England or other parts of the British Empire. Nearly half went to Canada, settling in Nova Scotia and

The financial state of France after the American Revolution led to the French Revolution in 1789. French civilians burned items related to nobility in protest.

Quebec. Some were offered land by the British government, but the loyalists would never recover what they had lost in the colonies.

Great Britain suffered the greatest loss. Its attempt to maintain control of all 13 colonies was a failure. More than 24,000 British soldiers died from battle and disease during the war. Thousands more had been wounded or taken prisoner. While Great Britain did manage to keep some of its North American land, mainly in Canada, it no longer ruled the 13 American colonies. Raw materials from the colonies now had to be acquired through formal trade agreements just as with any other independent nation. Colonial taxes and fees were no longer a source of income. That, along with the cost of the war, was a severe blow to the British economy.

Great Britain's failure became a success for the colonies. The patriots weren't able to achieve their original hope of equality with other British subjects, so they revised their goal to one of independence. It was a major victory. Thirteen separate colonies united to stand up to the British crown and achieved independence. There were terrible losses along the way—more than 16,000 American deaths from disease and battle. But inexperienced American soldiers managed to defeat a well-trained, professional British Army. The newly independent colonies had a long road ahead of them: building a government, recovering from the hardships of war, and establishing their place in the

Washington took the oath of office on April 30, 1789, to become the first president of the United States of America.

world community. But they could do so on their own terms, which was what they had been fighting for all along.

TIMELINE

November 1765—Parliament's Stamp Act goes into effect, and Americans boycott British goods

May 10, 1773—The Tea Act is passed; prices of British tea are lowered, but Americans still have to pay tax on it when it comes to shore

December 16, 1773—The Boston Tea Party takes place in Boston Harbor

March 1774—Parliament passes the Coercive Acts as punishment for the Boston Tea Party

September 5, 1774—The First Continental Congress assembles in Philadelphia

April 19, 1775—The first shots of the war are fired in Lexington, Massachusetts

May 10, 1775—The Second Continental Congress convenes and creates the Continental Army

June 17, 1775—The British suffer enormous losses at the Battle of Bunker Hill

July 4, 1776—Congress approves the Declaration of Independence

September 16, 1777—The British capture Philadelphia

February 6, 1778—France and the United States sign the Treaty of Alliance and the Treaty of Amity and Commerce

December 29, 1778—The British capture Savannah, Georgia

June 21, 1779—Spain joins the war as an ally of the American colonies and France

May 12, 1780—The British capture Charleston, South Carolina

October 7, 1780—The Continental Army defeats the British Army at Kings Mountain, South Carolina

January 17, 1781—The Continental Army earns a decisive victory against the British at the Battle of Cowpens

October 19, 1781—The British surrender at Yorktown, Virginia

September 3, 1783—The Treaty of Paris is signed, ending the war and ensuring American independence

GLOSSARY

ally—person or country united with another for a common purpose

amity—friendly relations between groups, such as nations

bankrupt—unable to pay debts

boycott—to refuse to buy or use a product or service to protest something believed to be wrong or unfair

casualties—people killed, wounded, or missing in a battle or in a war

confiscate—to take away something as punishment or to enforce the law or rules

conquer—to defeat and take control of an enemy

draft—a system that chooses people who are compelled by law to serve in the military

rebel—someone who fights against a government or the people in charge of something

rebellion—an armed revolt against a government

siege—military blockade of a city to cut off its supplies and force its surrender

supply line—the route used to deliver supplies, such as food, water, and equipment, to soldiers during a war

tanner—a person who prepares animal hides to be made into clothing and other goods

treason—the crime of betraying one's government

tyranny—unfair or brutal power

ADDITIONAL RESOURCES

Further Reading

Burgan, Michael. *The Untold Story of the Black Regiment: Fighting in the Revolutionary War.* North Mankato, Minn.: Compass Point Books, 2015.

Clarke, Gordon. *Significant Battles of the American Revolution.*
New York: Crabtree Publishing Company, 2013.

Rajczak, Kristen. *Life during the American Revolution.*
New York: Gareth Stevens Publishing, 2013.

Smith-Llera, Danielle. *The Presidency of George Washington: Inspiring a Young Nation.* North Mankato: Minn.: Compass Point Books, 2015.

Internet Sites

Use FactHound to find Internet sites related to this book. All of the sites on FactHound have been researched by our staff.

Here's all you do:

Visit *www.facthound.com*

Type in this code: 9780756551698

CRITICAL THINKING USING THE COMMON CORE

Identify the colonists' reasons for going to war in 1775. How did those reasons change over time? Why did they change? (Key Ideas and Details)

Imagine that France and Spain had decided to remain neutral during the war. Would the outcome of the revolution have changed? Why or why not? Support your explanation with details from the text. (Integration of Knowledge and Ideas)

Describe how the author structured the sequence of this book. Include examples of clues or cues that make the structure clear to the reader. Think about other ways the book could have been put together. Make a brief outline of an alternative structure. Explain how it would be understood differently by the reader. (Craft and Structure)

SOURCE NOTES

Page 9, pull quote: "The Boston Tea Party, 1773." EyewitnesstoHistory.com. 3 Feb. 2015. http://www. eyewitnesstohistory.com/teaparty.htm

Page 9, col. 2, line 17: T. H. Breen. *American Insurgents, American Patriots: The Revolution of the People.* New York: Hill and Wang, 2010, p. 61.

Page 18, pull quote: James Chalmers. "A Loyalist's Perspective on the Imperial Crisis." 18 Feb. 2015. http://people.sunyulster.edu/voughth/Candidus.htm

Page 18, col. 2, line 3: John Ferling. "Myths of the American Revolution." *Smithsonian Magazine.* January 2010. 9 Feb. 2015. http://www. smithsonianmag.com/ist/?next = /history/myths-of-the-american-revolution-10941835

Page 22, col. 2, line 11: *American Insurgents, American Patriots: The Revolution of the People,* p. 286.

Page 26, pull quote: Ibid., p. 42.

Page 40, pull quote: "Franklin's Contributions to the American Revolution as a Diplomat in France." Historic Valley Forge. 18 Feb. 2015. http://www. ushistory.org/valleyforge/history/franklin.html

SELECT BIBLIOGRAPHY

"The Boston Tea Party, 1773." EyewitnesstoHistory.com. 3 Feb. 2015. http://www.eyewitnesstohistory.com/teaparty.htm

Breen, T. H. *American Insurgents, American Patriots: The Revolution of the People.* New York: Hill and Wang, 2010.

Calloway, Colin G. "American Indians and the American Revolution." The American Revolution. National Park Service. 18 Feb. 2015. http://www.nps.gov/revwar/about_the_revolution/american_indians.html

Chalmers, James. "A Loyalist's Perspective on the Imperial Crisis." 18 Feb. 2015. http://people.sunyulster.edu/voughth/Candidus.htm

Ferling, John. "Myths of the American Revolution." *Smithsonian Magazine.* January 2010. 9 Feb. 2015. http://www.smithsonianmag.com/ist/?next=/history/myths-of-the-american-revolution-10941835

"Franklin's Contributions to the American Revolution as a Diplomat in France." Historic Valley Forge. 18 Feb. 2015. http://www.ushistory.org/valleyforge/history/franklin.html

"French Alliance, French Assistance, and European Diplomacy during the American Revolution, 1778–1782." Milestones: 1776–1783. U.S. Department of State Office of the Historian. 18 Feb. 2015. https://history.state.gov/milestones/1776-1783/french-alliance

Geist, Christopher. "A Common American Soldier." *Colonial Williamsburg Journal.* Autumn 2004. 18 Feb. 2015. http://www.history.org/foundation/journal/autumn04/soldier.cfm

"Hessians." George Washington's Mount Vernon. 18 Feb. 2015. http://www.mountvernon.org/research-collections/digital-encyclopedia/article/hessians

Lockhart, Paul. *The Whites of Their Eyes*: Bunker Hill, the First American Army, and the Emergence of George Washington. New York: Harper, 2011.

O'Shaughnessy, Andrew Jackson. *The Men Who Lost America*: British Leadership, the American Revolution and the Fate of the Empire. New Haven: Yale University Press, 2013.

"Revolution." *Africans in America.* 18 Feb. 2015. http://www.pbs.org/wgbh/aia/part2/2narr4_txt.html

Standiford, Les. *Desperate Sons: Samuel Adams, Patrick Henry, John Hancock, and the Secret Band of Radicals Who Led the Colonies to War.* New York: Harper, 2012.

Tonsetic, Robert L. *1781: The Decisive Year of the Revolutionary War.* Havertown, Pa.: Casemate Publishers, 2011.

"Treaty of Paris, 1783." Milestones: 1776–1783. U.S. Department of State Office of the Historian. 18 Feb. 2015. https://history.state.gov/milestones/1776-1783/treaty

Washburn, Wilcomb E. "Indians and the American Revolution." AmericanRevolution.org. 18 Feb. 2015. http://www.americanrevolution.org/ind1.html

INDEX

ABOUT THE AUTHOR

Kristin Marciniak writes the books she wishes she'd read in school. She has a degree in journalism from the University of Missouri–Columbia and lives in Kansas City, Missouri, with her husband, son, and golden retriever.